# A Little Book of
# *Forgiveness*

ALSO BY D. PATRICK MILLER

*The Book of Practical Faith*

*The Complete Story of the Course*

*News of a New Human Nature*

*Instructions of the Spirit:*
poems & intimations

*Love After Life*
(a novel)

*To the memory of my mother*

*who forgave me
for not writing a novel first*

# A
## *Little Book*
### of
# *Forgiveness*

≫≈

## Challenges & Meditations for Anyone with Something to Forgive

≫≈

## D. PATRICK MILLER

Fearless Books
Berkeley CA

Third Edition, Autumn 2004

FEARLESS BOOKS
2342 Shattuck Avenue #506
Berkeley CA 94704
*www.fearlessbooks.com*

*This book was originally published
in hardcover by Viking Penguin USA in 1994
and as a Fearless paperback in 1999*

Library of Congress
Cataloging-in-Publication Data
Miller, D. Patrick, 1953-
A little book of forgiveness : challenges and meditations
for anyone with something to forgive / D. Patrick Miller
Berkeley : Fearless Books, 2004
p.    cm.
"Tenth anniversary edition."
With a new foreword by Frederic Luskin.
ISBN 0-9656809-7-5
1. Forgiveness.    2. Forgiveness — Problems, exercises, etc.
3. Forgiveness — Meditations.    4. Forgiveness — Therapeutic use.
5. Interpersonal relations.    I. Title.    II. Luskin, Frederic
BF647.F67  M55  2004
158/.2 21

*Design & Typography by*
D. PATRICK MILLER

*(Cover based on original
design by Brian Mulligan)*

# CONTENTS

*Foreword*
by FREDERIC LUSKIN, PH.D.
*ix*

*Introduction*
I

SEVEN STEPS OF FORGIVING
5

FORGIVING OTHERS
15

FORGIVING YOURSELF
37

WHERE FORGIVENESS LEADS
67

*Acknowledgments*
91

# Foreword

WHEN first published in 1994, *A Little Book of Forgiveness* was a book whose ideas and message were ahead of its time. At that time there were only one or two published scientific studies demonstrating the power of forgiveness to make a difference in the lives of people who forgave. In 1994 my own thinking about forgiveness was mostly latent; I was unsure of just how important forgiveness was to the well-being of body and mind. I would not attempt my first research project until the end of 1996, and even then my thinking was rudimentary and lacking in power.

Since 1996 I have directed the Stanford Forgiveness Projects, a series of research endeavors that helped substantiate the power of forgiveness to reduce hurt, depression, anger and stress in people who hold grudges. In addition, the Forgiveness Projects have shown that forgiveness can reduce the physical manifestations of stress, reduce blood pressure in angry hypertensives, improve physical vitality and even improve one's compassion and optimism. The Projects have also shown that forgiveness is for everyone; we conducted research on hurt college students, angry and disappointed middle-aged adults, stressed-out business people, and people who have had family members murdered by political violence.

In addition to this research I also have taught forgiveness to literally thousands of hurt and angry people. What I find fascinating is that the things I taught, researched and proved to be true, D. Patrick Miller already knew. I am writing this foreword because of the remarkable degree of concordance *A Little Book of Forgiveness* has with the results of my research. The huge number of people I have worked with clinically demonstrate to me that the simple truths espoused in Mr. Miller's book are just that: simple truths.

One example of many is Mr. Miller's understanding of the power of gratitude. He writes this straightforward suggestion to establish the importance of this relationship: "To accelerate forgiveness, practice gratefulness." Then he goes on to describe the power of gratitude in his own life and how that has improved his ability to forgive. In our forgiveness methodology and my self-help book *Forgive for Good:*

*A Proven Prescription for Health and Happiness*, gratitude is a central concept. My experience has shown that the ability to feel gratitude is directly related to people's ability to forgive; grateful people seem to have an easier time letting go of their harsh judgments of people and events.

What I like about this book is I can pick it up at any page and get an insight that is helpful in both understanding and moving towards forgiveness. It does not matter where I begin or for what I am looking; each page resonates with some truth about the subject and is written in a gentle and inviting manner. It is clear that this book has emerged from personal experience and a depth of practice. Reading *A Little Book of Forgiveness* will offer the reader a safe and guided passage into a practice that is essential for mental and physical well-being. As Mr. Miller highlights so movingly, the more of us who practice forgiveness, the more people who are available to heal both our world and ourselves.

FREDERIC LUSKIN, PH.D.
Author, *Forgive for Good*
Director, Stanford Forgiveness Projects

# Introduction

W H E N I was a fledgling investigative reporter in my early twenties, I really wanted to save the world. In the simplest terms, my plan was to un-cover wrongdoing and make room for rightness to take its place. But it didn't take me long to realize that I could spend my whole life trying to expose the evil doings of "bad guys" and never answer the funda-mental question of human evil — that is, *what makes guys bad?*

Uncertain of how to blow the lid off *that* story, I decided that world-saving was too tough an assign-ment and set out to make a decent living instead. To shorten a decade-long story, that didn't work out so well either. When I was thirty-two my freelance career in graphic arts began to crash — along with my health, my closest relationships, and my pride — during a prolonged struggle with chronic fatigue immune deficiency syndrome (CFIDS).

But what I first perceived as a vicious insult of fate eventually proved to be a mighty blessing in disguise. The experience of profound psychological surrender induced by CFIDS was followed immediately by the deepest and most rapid learning of my adult life. As the spiritual longing that had always patiently abided at the edges of my awareness moved to center stage, a light was cast on the key to deliverance from suffering. This was the key that would renew my health, redeem my ways of relating, and reveal to me my true work as a writer.

That key is forgiveness. This little book is one result of my unplanned investigation into forgiveness since I became ill in 1985. Before that time, I thought forgiveness was a nice thing one did every now and then to let people off the hook for their stupidity or meanness — and to give oneself a fleeting feeling of warmth toward humanity in general. Now I understand that forgiveness is a radical way of life that openly contradicts the most common and popular beliefs of this troubled world. I also believe that it's the lack of forgiveness that "makes guys bad," spawning every kind of crime from the intimate to the global.

This work arose directly from my personal study and everyday experience of varied spiritual perspectives, including *A Course in Miracles*, Christianity, Buddhism, the *I Ching*, Sufism, Jungian psychology, and other influences too subtle to cite. The tone of these "challenges and meditations" is sometimes forceful not because I presume to lecture anyone, but because this is the voice I hear in my heart teaching me. I experience forgiveness as a provocative discipline, and so this is the way I am passing it on.

The first part of this book presents a specific prescription of how to go about any particular act of forgiving. The seven steps given are not the only way, but they provide a practical method that has proved reliable in my experience. In three somewhat arbitrary divisions, the rest of the book indicates how it may feel to adopt forgiving as a way of life. Feel free to read pages at random; ideas that are linked are marked with lower-case Roman numerals: *i, ii, iii.*

I hope readers can use these ideas the way I use them, as seeds for inspiration that lead to both personal and social change. I'm presenting what I've learned about forgiveness so far and forecasting where it may lead, but the particular messages I'm passing on are less important than the messages that readers receive while trying out this book. In a sense, I'm attempting to help others become *attuned to the frequency of forgiveness*: a clear tone of sane inner guidance in a world filled with the harsh static of fear, confusion, and vengeance.

At different times in my life I've tried to change the way that others thought and behaved, through journalism, creative expression, and argument. But only forgiveness has substantially changed *me* for the better — by making me less angry and self-absorbed, and thus better able to relate to people fairly and compassionately. I hope that the changes that have come through me also come through clearly in this book. If even a few readers are inspired to release some old and unforgiven pain in their lives, I will be a satisfied and ever more inspired activist.

# Seven Steps
of
Forgiving

I

Select a bitter sorrow, a serious grievance against someone, or a punishing charge against yourself, and review it in complete detail.

2

Hold in your mind the image of whatever is to be forgiven — yourself, another person, a past event — and say, "I release you from the grip of my sadness, disapproval, or condemnation." Concentrate quietly on this intention.

## 3

Imagine for a while what your life will be like without the sorrow or grievance that has been haunting you.

4

Make amends with someone you've hurt or someone who has hurt you; tell a friend about your self-forgiveness; or otherwise bring your inner work to your relationships.

Ask for God's help to overcome fear or resistance at any step. If you do not believe in God, ask for help from nature, humanity, and the mysteries of your own mind. These are the channels through which aid is sent — and aid is always sent.

6

Have patience. Forgiveness induces healing which follows its own order and timing. Whether you think you have accomplished anything thus far is less important than the fact that you have attempted a radical act that will call forth change likely to exceed your expectations. Go about your daily business, but stay alert to unexpected shifts in your thinking, feelings, and relationships.

Repeat steps 1 through 6 as often as necessary, for life.

# Forgiving
# Others

$I$T might seem a lot easier to forgive someone if only he or she would show signs of changing. The paradox is that we are unlikely to see signs of change in others until we have forgiven them. This is true for two reasons. First, resentment is blinding. It limits our perception of what is real (and changing) in the present, and shuts down our capacity to envision a happier future.

Second, a subtle but crucial function of forgiveness is that it tacitly gives others "permission" to change. We are not nearly so separate from each other as we generally experience ourselves to be. We think that we grow and change only within ourselves, but we also grow and change partly within others, and they within us. Some people may find very little space within themselves to change, and need others to let them into a psychic territory of forgiveness, where they can feel free to try a new way of living.

Soon after I had begun forgiving my parents for all the wrongs I thought they had done to me — without saying anything to them about it — it seemed that they suddenly became more open and frank about their personal history, everything that had influenced them to become who they were. At certain moments the extent of their revelations was stunning to me, and I wasn't sure of exactly what was happening. Had I heard these things before without paying attention, because of my resentments at the time? Or did my parents subconsciously feel permitted to tell me more about themselves because I was showing them subtle signs of greater acceptance than I ever had before?

Now I believe that both kinds of change were occurring, and this evolution continued. I'm no longer concerned about which was their change and which was mine. We all change together if we change at all. This overlapping of each other is easiest to experience in a couple, family, or other close relationship, but I suspect that it's true of the family of humanity as well.

That's what makes forgiveness so powerful. Anyone can initiate the changes we all need by opening up new territories within his or her mind — our one mind, really — where others can find the room to take a deep breath, start telling the truth, and shake off the cloak of guilt they have so long mistaken for their own skin.

Begin not with the idea that you are doing a favor to someone who hurt you, but that you are being merciful to yourself. To carry an anger against anyone is to poison your own heart, administering more toxin every time you replay in your mind the injury done to you. If you decline to repeat someone's offense *inwardly*, your *outward* anger will dissipate. Then it becomes much easier to tell the one who hurt you how things must change between you.

"Forgive and forget" is a popular distortion of the work of surrendering grievances. The real process is "Remember fully and forgive." If it were actually possible to forget everything you forgave, you could teach very little to others seeking freedom from their resentments.

*It's true that we do eventually forget some things we've truly forgiven. But that kind of forgetting takes care of itself; it's not something you can tell yourself or anyone else to do. Trying to forget is just another means of denial — and whatever is denied is not forgiven. Remembering fully helps us take note of what we do not want to see repeated, so that forgiveness doesn't inadvertently give anyone permission to commit the same mistakes again.*

When you are trying to decide whether someone deserves your forgiveness, you are asking the wrong question. Ask instead whether you deserve to become someone who consistently forgives.

Examine carefully the temptation to catalog, classify, and frequently update the file of wrongs done to you. The only case you will build is one against yourself, as you increasingly believe in secret that you deserve what you're getting, even as you complain about injustice.

Living in forgiveness means yielding your grip on misery. Many people feel that it is this grip that makes them authentic and serious; such is the melodrama of the adolescent soul. The adult soul empathizes with misery only to connect with those in suffering and lead them to forgiveness.

*When I was younger I spent a lot of time with friends commiserating — about the state of the world, the flaws and failures of people we knew, and everything else that added up to the general difficulty of being human. Now when I find myself drifting into pessimistic bull sessions, something new within me puts on the brakes and seeks a different, more useful direction for the conversation. I don't want to be a Pollyanna, skipping gaily off into a silly optimism and losing my connection with anyone who may still fully subscribe to the belief in suffering. I have to keep one foot planted there, at the ground level of another's unhappiness. But with the other foot I try, sometimes awkwardly, to step up or out in a new direction. Sometimes I think I might be a better exemplar of hope if I were more confident of where I'm going. But it's possible that people are moved more by another's tentative willingness to see things differently than they would be by a dramatic declaration of a better way. Perhaps watching someone learn to change makes a more lasting impression than having someone try to save you.*

Forgiveness may be stern or soft, reassuring or discomforting, eloquent or clumsy. The first expression may be incomplete and need restatement or elaboration to be understood by others, and made clear and strong in one's own heart. Sainthood is not a prerequisite for attempting to forgive.

"Sweet revenge" is junk food for the soul. The brief rush that revenge provides will always be followed by the degradation of one's character. There is a real joy to be found in setting things right, but that always involves changing oneself for the better first.

To find your missing creativity, release a little of your attachment to the worst injury ever done to you. Grieve the deadness that you are letting go of, and that you have so long regarded as a trophy wound. Then celebrate the opening of a door through which your childlike nature can come back to you, laughing, asking the simplest questions, clearing your vision.

*In a time when the recollection and cataloging of abuses done to people has become a virtual industry, we have to be careful about proclaiming the specialness of our wounds. The end point of remembering exactly how we have been damaged is to realize that we all share the deep common wound of humanity: being born into vulnerable bodies in a mysterious and dangerous world. Our particular wounds have a lot to do with who we are, and that history is important to understand. But learning to forgive all our wounds, regardless of their severity, is what will speed us toward our potential. An unimagined creativity blossoms in every space within the heart from which pain has been released.*

Forgiveness is the first breeze of early spring, carrying an unexpected warmth.

Don't be alarmed when resentment returns after you think you have thoroughly released someone from blame. Our attachment to fear runs deep, and the thought of holding no grudges whatsoever loosens fear's grip. Then it whispers in our ear that forgiveness might steal away our old familiar world of isolation and suspicion. Whenever you find a good reason to reinforce an old grievance, ask yourself what fear has actually done for you lately.

In the forgiving relationship, the struggle over power is replaced by the mutual impetus to serve. Jealousy dissolves into playfulness, suspicion into helpfulness, and possession into shared freedom.

*Early in our relationship my wife and I struggled through an unusual pattern of conflict. Each of us rushed to take more blame for our problems in communicating: "I'm causing more trouble than you are"; "No, I am!" I don't know if this was easier than blaming each other in the conventional fashion, but it did lead us to the capacity to allow each other to fail at crucial moments. Accepting that we both fail, and will fail, is what might be called proactive forgiveness. This allows us to see our marriage as a mutual learning process instead of a battle over "getting our needs met." As we glimpse that learning to love is our fundamental need, it's easier to be patient about each other's tendencies that might otherwise be intolerable in the short term. Thus we are able to live and relate with less and less anger, and work steadily toward a constant and creative joy in our relationship — but without any deadlines.*

The most efficient expression of forgiveness answers attack just as it happens, neither by condoning nor opposing it, but by staunchly offering correction of its senselessness.

*i*

A robber steals because he thinks something has been stolen from him. If we hope to rehabilitate him, rather than reinforce his violent habit, the message of our rehabilitation efforts must be: "*Things are not as they seem; you have everything you need within you.*" Anyone trapped in illusion is healed by seeing through it, not by being schooled in a harsher illusion. Thus, all criminals need a better metaphysics, a wiser foundation for their thinking.

*ii*

How to forgive a murderer? First, by differentiating his sufferings from his exploitation of death to ease them. For his sufferings — greed, jealousy, frustration — he will need re-education, support, and compassion. For our outrage about murder, we need to examine deeply our faith in death. As long as we collectively believe that death has power over life, we will spawn deluded, self-appointed little gods who want that power.

If you want to be merciless, be merciless against the temptation to blame. Question the usefulness of blaming at every opportunity. Ask yourself, "If I had committed a crime, would I respond better to condemnation or caring?" If you find within yourself a secret desire to be condemned, question its logic before relying on it any longer as a basis for decision-making and relationship.

*i*

Make no mistake: anyone or anything that seems to have control over you is experienced as a momentary stand-in for God. Every grievance, regardless of degree, is an argument with divine creation, the fundamental power that made things the way they are. In other words: *When you are mad at anyone you are mad at God.* When you are mad at God, it is crucially important to admit it. This saves many potential victims from your anger, redirecting it toward Someone who can transform it and heal you.

*ii*

It is difficult to stay mad at God, because most of the time our experience of God is nothing more than an idea. *Yet our consciousness itself is nothing more than an endless rush of ideas about reality.* In this view, for-giving God means exchanging many useless ideas for one idea that works.

*The grudge against God — or in nonreligious terms, the grudge against reality — is the keystone grudge for all of one's unhappiness. I've learned that I can save a lot of time by following the connections of all my petty, middling, and major grudges back to the keystone grudge, and then asking myself the question, "Is it more likely that God was wrong to make the world this way, or that I am somehow wrong in the way I'm looking at it?" If I decide that God was wrong — or that there is no God and I am merely the vic-tim of an uncaring, mechanical universe — then there isn't much I can do. But when I realize that I can always clari-fy my perceptions of the world, I can start learning and contributing again. That seems to be the way to both humility and power.*

# Forgiving
# Yourself

*I* HAVE *experienced two fundamental ways of being in the world. Until I became ill in my early thirties, I lived the normal life of ego: looking out for No. 1, trying to preserve my habits and defend my fixed worldview, and making bargains with my fears in order to squeeze some enjoyment out of life. In this consciousness everything felt risky and there were few people I trusted. But I could always compare myself to someone less fortunate and feel like I was making out all right.*

*After the physical and psychological crisis that devastated my former sense of self, I found myself on a spiritual path, whether I meant to end up there or not. This meant that I couldn't focus on looking out for No. 1, because I wasn't sure of who or what I was anymore (or even if an "I" exists at all!). It meant entering a never-ending discipline of surrendering my habits and enlarging my worldview in the light of new information and insights. Finally, it meant regarding fear as a common illusion — something to be acknowledged honestly but never allowed to dictate terms.*

*In this consciousness I increasingly feel cared for, by an ineffable, pervasive intelligence that I sometimes call God, and sometimes don't need to name at all. And I* trust everyone to be doing the best they can to find that same kind of security, even if some are seriously misguided or tragically deluded in their pursuit of it.

In a day-to-day sense, I don't know if my spiritual way of life is any easier than my old ego-driven way. In some respects it's more demanding. What has made the shift worthwhile is that my life makes sense to me now, and I feel consistently guided toward growth and service. In the old life I deeply doubted my worth and purpose, and secretly thought that I had too many insoluble problems to be of real help to anyone.

The bridge from my old life to the new was forgiveness: the complete release of my pained idea of who I was. This is the most important work I have ever done on my own behalf. In retrospect I marvel at the victory I was earning during the time that I felt I was suffering a total, grinding defeat.

Begin with the dull ache of a long-held shame. Don't try to argue away its justification; you've lost that argument many times already. Accept that your shame has helped make you who you are. Then compare your present sense of self to your sense of who you could be, who you've always wished to be, who you were born to be before you collided with the inevitable limitations and contradictions of this world. Between your shame and your ideal vision of yourself lies a great longing. Shift your attention to that longing — and look back on your unforgiven shame. This is the first step out of pain and stagnation.

Forgiving your flaws and failures does not mean looking away from them or lying about them. Look at them as a string of pitiful or menacing hitchhikers whom you can't afford *not* to pick up on your journey to a changed life. Each of them has a piece of the map you need hidden in its shabby clothing. You must listen attentively to all their stories and win the friendship of each one to put your map together. Where you are going — into a forgiven life of wholeness, passion, and commitment — you will need all the denizens of your dark side working diligently on your behalf.

*i*

A rage of frustration boiled over and you struck, changing your life and someone else's forever. There is an insult or injury you dealt that cannot be taken back or dismissed. This seems to be proof of your sinfulness, the personal stain that won't ever wash out. In fact it is the dye of your initiation into a more serious life. If you continue to live on automatic, you will do more damage. You must now learn to pay profound attention to your inner workings, which mirror the workings of the world at large. You must become an eminently practical, everyday philosopher of pain and redemption, changing your habits and exemplifying change for others as you go along. This is the work you chose for yourself when you attacked. It only begins with apologies and recompense.

*ii*

When did you decide that you had the power to ruin your whole life? How do you know how much healing is possible? Are you in charge of all creation? Are you calling all the shots?

*When I began to understand how arrogant it was to believe that I was doomed, I was chagrined in a way I had never felt before. What was new was that this particular chagrin did not add to my burden of shame, but only helped dissolve it. To forgive myself I had to see clearly my errors of thinking and then truly release them, which meant giving up the expectation that I would continue to think stupidly.*

*My habitual, circular thinking of shame and negativity stopped when I realized that it's not just myself doing the thinking that counts. At my best I'm just translating creativity from a source beyond my comprehension. (Is there anyone who can describe exactly how they get an idea, and precisely where it comes from?) By keeping the channel of creativity as free as possible of shame, blame, doubt, and fear, I can achieve far more than I ever could by deliberate, rational efforts. Giving up the notions that I knew exactly who I was, and how great my failures were, actually enabled me to take charge of my life and better manage the creativity that comes through me.*

Self-hatred is nearly universal and takes many forms, from arrogance to false humility. Forgiveness teaches that we need not actually learn to "love ourselves" but instead to see that everything hateful or unloving within us is a tragic fiction that can be gently, firmly set aside. When there is nothing left within us *but* love, then forgiveness has brought us to reality.

Never forget that to forgive yourself is to release trapped energy that could be doing good work in the world. Thus, to judge and condemn yourself is a form of selfishness. Self-prosecution is never noble; it does no one a service.

Forgiveness induces a *feeling* of release, but it is actually a logical process — for you will not let go of the lamented past until you understand that continuing its suffering into the future is pointless.

Forgiveness feels most dramatic when some ancient pattern of self-punishment collapses in a torrent of tears. But it is just as effective when practiced daily in tiny doses — relinquishing a pointless worry, getting wise to a self-destructive habit, serving notice on a cruel notion about yourself that has previously seemed justified. The beginning of forgiveness is alertness to false ideas.

*The essence of forgiveness is release, and only that which is false needs to be released. That's how I use forgiveness as an inner tool of self-development, constantly paring away the false from the true, the muddy from the clear, the destructive from the useful. Applied to one's own consciousness, forgiveness is a sharp knife of discernment, and it may rapidly surpass the effects of countless hours of sit-down meditation or religious ritual. You have only to be willing to slice away the illusory roots of your personality, and briefly grieve the passing of the distorted images you have so long lived by. Then a new life, less limited by destructive habits and prejudices, can surface within you.*

If your first attempts at self-forgiveness seem to change nothing in the way you feel, you are impatient for magic. Like an incantation, the steps of forgiving yourself may need many solemn repetitions before a door in your mind opens to real change. The change happens within you but comes from beyond you; you are only the Magician's helper.

*i*

Don't be fooled by the subtlety of some self-punishments, and do not mistake what is habitual for what is natural. Brooding, resenting, feeling bored, and frequently reviewing your laundry list of grumbles may seem like innocent reactions to a cruel world. In fact these are all ways in which your attention wanders from the purpose of healing, the only worthwhile work in the world.

*ii*

Forgiveness brings order to your mind because it is the commitment to see everything — pain or pleasure, love or hatred, disaster or victory — in terms of the healing potential within. This decision is the key to a deep, abiding happiness that can sustain you through all passing sadnesses.

Forgiveness is a long night walk by the ocean at ebb tide, with the surf only murmuring.

*i*

Bad habits linger because they are unforgiven, not because one lacks willpower. Forgiving begins with appreciating the seriousness of the struggle that goes on while changing a habit. Your old familiar self will seldom yield gracefully to a new emerging one. To forgive a bad habit, never think of it as petty; changing a habit is actually the struggle to choose between a world of hurt and a world of healing. Paying exquisite attention will eventually enable you to let go of the deadening past, and rejoin the flow of your real life.

*ii*

Every addiction is rooted in reluctance to shed some of the personality's coat of armor. The more willing we are to forgive our own defenses, the more spirit can come rushing in through the gaps in our armor.

*iii*

To become completely free of addictions would be to lose all the barriers that separate us from each other. But don't worry about losing your personality; forgiveness will never rob you of what you truly need. As you discover that you prefer the feelings of freedom to those of self-defense, your capacity to handle freedom will increase.

To accelerate forgiveness, practice gratefulness. Every night, try to give equal thanks for all the day's events and encounters. When you discover yourself becoming grateful for things that seemed unpleasant when they occurred, you will be breaking the bonds of ordinary personality. You will soon no longer need to take pride in your wounds as a defense.

*I was astonished when I began to positively appreciate my defeats, downturns, and disappointments. The sooner they were forgiven — that is, the sooner I gave up looking at them in only one way — the more quickly my misfortunes seemed to add to my strength, alertness, and responsibility. As I began to perceive disappointment in a brighter light, I had to admit that "good" and "bad" events were getting harder and harder to tell apart. Lately it seems that bad things are merely those which I'm not yet prepared to handle effectively — and it also seems that they present themselves in order to help me increase my competence.*

Forgiveness broadens your point of view and gives you see-through vision. Forgiveness floods your tiny resources of logic and rationality with an ocean of inspiration. You need only surrender the jealous guarding of your favorite, familiar frustrations.

Forgiveness replaces the need to anticipate fearfully with the capacity to accept gracefully and improvise brilliantly. It does not argue with fate, but recognizes the opportunities latent within it. If necessity is the mother of invention, forgiveness is the midwife of genius.

Learning is slowed less by lack of intelligence than by a reluctance to let go of bankrupt ideas and exhausted ways of seeing. This is why some problems never seem to go away even when their solutions are clearly within our grasp. When you feel cursed by fate, look to your own stubbornness; when you seem blocked by others' stupidity, question your own reasoning and the way you communicate. When nothing seems to work, consider whether you have correctly identified the fundamental problem behind your struggles. The *object* of your blame will always prove to be less of an obstacle than your *decision* to blame.

Forgiveness gradually enables you to deal directly and fully with all of your experiences and relationships, instead of cutting off those that threaten pain or humiliation. In this sense, forgiveness is the key to versatility and openness.

Failure of the body provides a great temptation not to forgive, because forgiving may not soon halt the body's suffering. To understand this difficulty we must remember that *the body itself is the first disability each of us experiences,* and we have been angry with it ever since we were born hungry and wanting. Some religions reinforce this anger, warning that the body will demean our spirit unless it is punished and controlled. But not even the body can be convicted of wrongdoing on the basis of less than all the facts, and we live in a world rife with illusion and speculation. Learning to forgive the body may not cure our individual ills, but it will hasten the healing of the human condition. Anyone who learns to bear the body's suffering without anger is a noble missionary indeed.

*ii*

Forgiveness effectively uses the body for communication, and frees the body from being misused as an argument for loneliness.

Attack upon the body is a distorted attempt to liberate the spirit, and glorification of the body is misplaced praise of the spirit. Forgiveness corrects both errors without punishment.

The forgiven life is neither simple nor untroubled, and forgiveness does not prevent unexpected misfortunes. With practice, forgiveness does reduce the severity and frequency of those misfortunes that we tend to arrange for ourselves.

When you first decide to forgive yourself you are stepping upon a great escalator headed up toward your potential. If you later decide to turn back you will only stay where you are, until your renewed efforts at self-condemnation prove too exhausting to continue. If you decide to increase the escalator's pace with further efforts to understand and forgive yourself, you will see the gladdening sights up ahead just that much sooner.

# Where
# Forgiveness
# Leads

C A N *we begin to imagine a politics of forgiveness? We've had the politics of one-upmanship, deception, and belligerence for so long that we may mistake this way of doing things for "human nature." If we believe that we must fight against our own nature to change our politics, then peace, justice, and human equality become romantic ideals that can never be achieved — although they can always be used as excuses for more war and sacrifice, to keep the enormous wheels of global misery grinding along.*

*The extent to which we think "world peace" is possible is exactly the extent to which we think our own minds can someday be peaceful through and through. If we cannot understand why warring nations fight over territories, national pride, or religious beliefs, then we need look for insight no further than our fight for a parking space, the struggle to procure a prestigious position over our competitors, or the aggressive ministry to convert one more soul to our church.*

*But human nature encompasses more than our destructive habits; it also has within it the potential for surrender. If we think of surrender as raising the white flag before our enemies, nothing within us will change.*

The surrender that matters is giving up the belief that we have any enemies. It doesn't matter whether humanity achieves that surrender tomorrow or a thousand years from now; simply remembering to make the attempt whenever possible is what will eventually undo the world as we know it.

How could our politics begin to express forgiveness? Imagine politicians debating publicly in order to learn from each other and educate the public, striving to outdo each other only on the attempt to make sure all parties have been fairly heard. Imagine the media hesitating in its rush to judgment of people and events — hesitating in order to place their reporting in the context of the most profound questions of human consciousness and moral evolution. Imagine our country's diplomatic envoys arguing for peace in international venues by admitting our warring history and tendencies first.

Are these radical departures from politics-as-usual really beyond human nature? Not if they are within our imagining — and if we can couple our imagination with an intense desire to end the human habit of alienation.

Forgiveness is one of the most undersold propositions of all time. When you first begin to grasp the potential of forgiveness, you will cheerfully trade all prior investments in aggression for the peace of its action.

Forgiveness blossoms at a certain moment in time, when you are ripe and ready to release some of the dead past. *It is the intent to forgive that actually speeds up time*, collapsing old schedules of suffering and bringing unimagined possibilities inestimably nearer.

Every act of forgiveness has the same nature and a unique expression. Your challenge is to create your particular style of forgiveness, and then take it on the road.

Forgiveness unifies one's own awareness and will unite the consciousness of all humankind, which has been so long shattered into opposing egos, cultures, religions, and ideologies. Yet forgiveness also allows a creative diversity of ideas within one's own mind and instills a passionate tolerance of others' opinions and beliefs. Forgiveness will eventually preside over the raucous house-of-commons of the human soul, leading it with rigorous benevolence toward home.

Do not be misled by the myriad political faces of simple, stupid hatred. Jews and Arabs hating each other, Irish and Englishmen hating each other, whites and blacks, Christians and Muslims, leftists and rightwingers — there is no reason or dignity to any of it. Every chronic hatred began when someone attacked, someone suffered, and no one forgave. Then these insane examples were multiplied and unwisely taught down through the generations, falsely ennobled in tales of crusades, uprisings, and martyrdom. *But the cycle of vengeance will never resolve itself.* Someone has to step outside the cycle and courageously say, "I will take no pride in my tradition as long as it teaches murder, sacrifice, or revenge."

Beware also of hating the man who hates. Remember that you are here to help him lift off his yoke, not to boast that you stagger under one of a nobler design.

*I've always been amazed by the power of bigots or hate-mongers to arouse within me precisely the kind of hatred I despise within them. This is their real (if subconscious) agenda — not to further their race, culture, or beliefs, but to clone their inward misery in the consciousness of others, and thus feel less alone. Ultimately this is a self-defeating strategy, but it gains a little credence every time the hater can inspire any kind of hatred within another person, regardless of whether it's a hatred that supports or opposes his cause. To understand the hater, I need look no further than my revulsion in his presence. And I have to look at this revulsion steadily, continuously, courageously — until I see exactly how my own loneliness has crafted such a fearsome mask. Then I am a step closer to understanding how bigotry might be undone.*

Forgiveness does not mean letting error and evil continue unchecked, but it does require us to help each other trace all our errors to their source: the idea that we have been abandoned here to die. In countless forms this idea creates all the despair of the world. By striving to surrender the belief in abandonment, anyone can practice resurrection.

Anger exiles hope to the mind's dark and stuffy attic, cluttered with nostalgic curiosities. Forgiveness clears a space in the mind where hope finds enough room to devise practical strategies of change.

Forgiveness sends a healing message much further than you might believe. As you develop a forgiving demeanor you become an automatic transmitter within the network of human consciousness — changing minds less by your words than by your example, saving souls less by your program than by your presence.

A conviction is a strong and fixed belief; to be convicted is to be found guilty of something. There is more than a semantic connection between belief and guilt. Whenever we believe we know something for sure in this uncertain, paradoxical world, we will be perilously close to convicting ourselves or others of unpardonable crimes. Forgiveness gradually and carefully relieves us of our dependence on believing, increasingly enabling us just to be. Then our actions can arise from an instinctive wisdom that draws from our practical knowledge, yet transcends our limited grasp of truth.

Forgiveness is a curious paradox of accepting everything just as it is while working tirelessly for a complete upheaval in our behavior and consciousness. Some believe we must be constantly aggrieved to set right the injustices of the world — that good anger corrects bad anger. But an enlightened activism respectfully acknowledges all anger and sorrow while demonstrating the superior strategy of mercy, pooling ever deeper within and rhythmically flowing without. The most effective and lasting action arises from profound stillness and radical clarity.

Ultimately, forgiveness means letting go of this world, a darkened, fractured glass through which we see love only dimly. As our frightened grip on all that is temporary relaxes, we will increasingly find our authentic strength in that which is timeless, bound-less, inexhaustible, and omnipresent. *Heaven is learned*, not simply entered with religion's passport.

Forgiveness is not mere sympathy, nor condescension, nor forced generosity. It is the ultimate declaration of equality, founded on the recognition that all crimes are the same crime, every failing the human failing, and every insult a cry for help.

*The only way to remain angry at someone is to stop thinking about what may have caused that person to perpetuate a crime or injury. Because if you thoroughly investigate people's motivations, you will eventually find the sense, however twisted, behind all destructive acts. It will boil down to one of two general purposes: Either people think that causing others suffering will ease their own, or they believe that everyone deserves only suffering. These mistaken beliefs drive the world as we know it, and I doubt that anyone is entirely free of them. When I recognize these errors in myself or someone who tempts my anger, I try to remember that I want to learn and teach something new. I can hardly judge or punish others for their mixed-up motivations before I have completely straightened out my own.*

Forgiveness is a strong steady rain washing away drought.

*i*

A shock is felt when you realize that you have mistaken cynicism for sophistication, and that very little of what you have so long and bitterly believed is true. For you have hoarded only the evidence that fit your theories of attack and served to preserve your misery. In your changing vision, all that evidence is evaporating like a mist. This can be highly embarrassing — what if your friends see you losing all your vaunted toughness? But forgiveness doesn't particularly care about your social reputation.

Or you think you are always gentle, yet look at how viciously the world strikes at you nonetheless! This idea of your victimization is merely cynicism turned inside out and made more impenetrable to insight. You are clever enough to disguise your addiction to gloom in protests of innocence. The good news is that you may never be effectively challenged by others about this routine; few friends have enough wisdom and chutzpah at the same time. The bad news is that you will probably never walk your way to forgiveness in sensible steps. You will have to leap your own well-built defenses, disowning your morbid vanity in mid-flight.

Forgiveness is the science of the heart: a discipline of discovering all the ways of being that will extend your love to the world, and discarding all the ways that do not.

*i*

As forgiveness liberates your energy, you may be moved to sing, dance, write, make art, or otherwise celebrate. Don't let your day job get in the way.

As forgiveness liberates your thinking, you may find yourself looking beyond the world-wearying drives of self-promotion and competition. Congratulations! Now you are consciously evolving, no longer running the treadmill of humanity's favorite follies. Now you will be led by inspiration everywhere you are needed.

# ACKNOWLEDGMENTS

T H E thoughts in this book draw on every relationship I've ever experienced, so to thank everyone who's played a part in its development would be an impossible task. I will mention those who most recently contributed, and hope that the rest may find a way to forgive me (see Part I). For reading and commenting on the manuscript, I'd like to thank my parents, Lester and Janie Miller; my psychological mentor, Tom Rusk MD; Ann Lyon-Boutelle; J. Ruth Gendler; Billie Fitzpatrick; and especially Laurie Fox — my wife, editor, and agent, all in one exceptionally aesthetic package. Linda Chester, founder of the agency Laurie works with, genuinely took this work to heart and skillfully navigated the shoals and whirlpools of Manhattan's publishing world to help find the book its first home at Viking. There, editor Caroline White accurately saw how the original draft could be improved, and her insights and guidance still grace the current edition.

In preparing, producing, and marketing two Fearless editions of this work, I have been immeasurably assisted by typographer Linda Davis; the folks providing prepress proofs at Canterbury Press in Berkeley; Tim Wertheimer, Gabe Watts, and the whole crew at Data Reproductions in Auburn Hills, MI; and finally Gail Kump, Eric Kampmann, Chris Bell, and Julie Hardison of Midpoint Trade Books.